Have Her Over for Dinner

a gentleman's guide to classic, simple meals

Matt Moore

Nashville, TN

Last Resort Press books are available through most bookstores, via Ingram Distribution. Substantial discounts on bulk quantities of Last Resort Press books are available by contacting the sales department at Last Resort Press at the email address provided below.

Nashville, TN
lastresortpress@gmail.com
Manufactured in the United States of America
ISBN # (13) 978-0-615-31879-0
ISBN # (10) 0615318797

Professional photography and cover shot by Paige Rumore
All other photography by Matt Moore
Graphic design by Jill Townsend

*Author has received no compensation for any brand recommendations or product placements. Suggested brands and featured products are provided by recommendation only and do not constitute any other relationship.

10 9 8 7 6 5 4 3 2 1

TO MOM:
FOR ALWAYS LETTING ME HANG AROUND IN *YOUR* KITCHEN!

WOMEN LOVE A MAN WHO CAN COOK. ODDS ARE IF YOU ARE HOLDING THIS BOOK IN YOUR HAND, YOU ARE PROBABLY ONE OF THOSE WHO CANNOT. NO PROBLEM. I'VE BEEN IN YOUR SHOES BEFORE. I didn't create this book to show you how to "win" the girl of your dreams or prepare foods to ensure a "hookup." Instead, I want to help you tackle a problem that comes along in any relationship ... having her over for dinner. Let's face it. Not much effort goes into taking her out for a fancy dinner. Sure, you might reserve the restaurant, make a few recommendations, and hand over the credit card, but, at the end of the night, your creativity is on par with just about every other guy out there. A major part of earning her attention is setting yourself apart. Relax; you don't have to be a professional athlete, a famous actor, or insanely wealthy to catch her interest. All you need is a reasonably equipped kitchen, some quality ingredients, and a plan. Before we get started, I've got to come clean on one thing: I am not a chef.

Having said that, I should say that cooking has been a passion of mine most of my life. In our family, you might even call it an obsession. As a kid growing up in my home, I often complained that we always had dinner around the dining room table instead of at the local pizza joint like most of my friends. Looking back now, I realize just how meaningful and important those experiences were in my life. Beyond being fortunate enough to have a strong, close-knit family, dinner was always a learning experience. For just as my grandmother passed along generations of culinary knowledge to my mother, my mother instilled in us an appreciation and an understanding of the importance of great ingredients, simple preparation, and artful presentation.

The fact that I am not a chef is one very critical aspect of this book. Just like you, I get tired of reading recipes written by chefs that feature dozens of ingredients which can only be found in high-end food stores. Don't get me wrong, great chefs and fine dining definitely have their place in the world; however for most of us, their recipes and techniques are too expensive and complex to try and emulate at home.

It wasn't until college that I began to get really serious about my cooking. College provided the perfect setting for me to spend countless hung-over mornings lounging on the sofa watching cooking shows instead of attending class. As time passed, I began to really take the time to understand ingredients and develop the skills and techniques needed to create and perfect my recipes. Thinking back, what better learning environment could I have had: Funds were low, space was limited, and time was always short. Little did I know that I was building my story for the pages that follow.

For better or for worse, word about my talent in the kitchen spread fast. I was always the guy who was volunteered to handle the cooking for every occasion ... parties, date nights, sporting events. Later on, friends would often call on me when they needed help impressing a new girl, calming the storm in a turbulent relationship, or simply when the "eating out routine" became a bore. The sentiment was always the same: "Give me something easy that I can handle without all of the bullshit." I'd usually try to stick to recipes that focused on quality ingredients rather than on quantity, and I believe you'll find that simple idea to be the central theme throughout this book.

My goal is to provide you with the essential skills necessary to use simple preparation to turn quality ingredients into outstanding meals that she *and you* will savor. Cooking can be quite enjoyable, so this is not a book that directs you to open this, heat that, and serve. Hopefully, this book will teach you that beyond the somewhat snobby façade of the cooking industry, its contents are fairly straightforward. However, like anything worth pursuing, practice and preparation will be necessary. I have included instructions for making items from scratch without having a grocery list a mile long. I also realize that there are certain times that you won't have time to make a homemade pasta sauce or a salad dressing, so I will provide my favorite store brands that can be substituted without blowing your cover.

Think about it this way: Women and food are essential to survival, happiness, health, and overall well being. Aside from impressing that lovely lady, you may discover that you have talents you didn't know you possessed. I am confident you will be able to master all of these techniques and recipes.

NOW, CRACK OPEN A BEER, AND LET'S GET TO WORK.

THIS BOOK IS ABOUT TEACHING THE BASICS OF COOKING, WITHOUT REQUIRING DOZENS OF INGREDIENTS OR EXPENSIVE EQUIPMENT TO COMPLETE THE MEALS.

Recipes are geared towards natural, fresh items that require little manipulation in order to taste and look good.

The majority of the meals are well-balanced and feature healthy ingredients, yet they remain cost conscious. In addition, the ingredients used in these recipes are consistent throughout the book. I don't have you running out to purchase one expensive item that you will never use again. This will help save time and money as you progress through the dinners. Nearly all of the ingredients are very accessible and can be found in most large grocery stores located throughout the country.

The theme of this book focuses on entire meals, rather than just individual recipes. Full "menus" are presented to accompany each entrée, but it's up to you to decide if you want to make everything, or just the entrée. Essentially, I'm putting the control in your hands.

I'm not a chef. I can't emphasize that point enough. I know how challenging it can be in the kitchen without much experience. I'm giving you instructions and directions, man to man, without the attitude. All of these recipes have been tested and duplicated by guys just like you. Hopefully you will find some humor, sarcasm, and a laid-back approach to my writing that will help you succeed in the pages that follow.

The Basics

cooking defined, ingredients, and equipment

I HATE DEFINITIONS JUST AS MUCH AS THE NEXT GUY. Because of that, I try my best not to use too many fancy terms in my recipes. That being said, I promised you would learn something by reading this book. Some of these terms need to be committed to memory for future reference in the kitchen. Look at it this way, a major part of any relationship is learning how to compromise. I'll do my part and try and keep things basic, but if you come across something that you don't understand, do your part and refer back to these terms.

AL DENTE - term used to describe cooked pasta, rice, or vegetables. Al dente is firm to the bite but not hard; a slight resistance occurs when chewed.

BAKE - to cook by dry heat, especially in an oven.

BRAISE - to cook slowly in fat and moisture (stock, broth, wine, water) in a closed pot.

BROIL - to cook by direct exposure to high heat.

CHIFFONADE - to stack, roll, and finely slice greens or herbs into long thin strips.

COMPOUND BUTTER - a butter with added components (flavor and/or ingredients).

DEGLAZE - to dissolve the small particles of sautéed solids remaining in a pan by adding liquid and heating.

DIRECT HEAT - to cook by direct exposure to the heat source.

DRESS - to season and/or add dressing to a salad or greens.

EMULSIFY - to convert two or more immiscible liquids. Oil and vinegar, for example.

FRY - to cook in a pan or in a griddle over heat with the use of fat or oil.

GARNISH - to add decorative or savory touches to enhance presentation or taste.

GRILL - to broil on a grill.

INDIRECT HEAT - to cook by offsetting the heat source from the food.

JULIENNE - to cut into long thin strips of the same size and thickness.

KOSHER SALT - a natural form of salt that is larger in grain and more subtle in flavor. Table salt can be substituted; 1 unit of Table Salt to 1½ units of Kosher Salt is generally a good rule for conversion.

ON THE BIAS - to cut diagonally, across the grain.

PARMIGIANO REGGIANO - a variety of Parmesan cheese that is of higher quality and from a select region in Italy. Domestic varieties of fresh Parmesan cheese can be substituted when necessary, but try to avoid that stuff in the green canister whenever possible.

PLATE - to arrange food on a plate, platter, or serving surface.

ROUX - flour and fat (oil or butter) mixture used as a thickening agent, especially in Cajun cuisine.

SAUTÉ - to fry in a small amount of fat or oil.

"TO TASTE" - to add seasonings or ingredients suited to your preference, especially salt.

WHISK - to use a quick light brushing or whipping motion.

Photos (left) shot at Lazzaroli Pasta, Nashville, TN

IF YOU ARE LLOYD CHRISTMAS *FROM DUMB & DUMBER,* the bare essentials would refer to a case of beer, an oversized foam cowboy hat, a pin wheel, a paddle ball, and a *Rhode Island Slut* magazine ... Since we're talking about your kitchen here, it's best to always keep the following ingredients on hand. **To make shopping easier, these ingredients are marked by an * in the following recipes to indicate that you should already have these stocked in your kitchen.** That is of course, assuming you are paying any attention whatsoever.

OILS AND VINEGAR –
keep in a cool, dry place; 6 months to 1 year
Balsamic Vinegar
Red Wine Vinegar
Extra Virgin Olive Oil

DRIED SPICES AND HERBS –
keep in cool, dry place; 6 months
Kosher Salt
Pepper
Garlic Powder
Oregano
Cajun Seasoning
Herbs de Provence or Italian Blend Seasoning
Red Pepper Flakes

CONDIMENTS –
refrigerate after opening, follow product instructions
Soy Sauce
Whole Grain Mustard
Ketchup
Mayonnaise

FRESH ITEMS
Garlic – *1 month refrigerated; 2 - 3 weeks in a cool, dry place*
Unsalted butter – *2 - 3 months refrigerated; freeze and thaw as needed up to 6 months*
Eggs – *3 - 4 weeks refrigerated*
Lemons – *2 weeks refrigerated; 5 - 7 days in a cool, dry place*
Fresh Herbs (Basil, Parsley) **–** *5 - 6 days refrigerated; 3-4 days in a cool, dry place. A potted plant of herbs is always a good option.*

Photos (left) shot at the Nashville Farmers Market

SURE, HAVING EVERY NIFTY GADGET AND TOOL UNDER THE SUN IS WHAT DEFINES US AS MEN, but for most of us, it's not realistic. All of the following recipes can be made by using some combination of the equipment listed here. Don't worry; I'm very careful to cue you in on what's needed for each recipe. I've also given you my thoughts on a few items to help you out. Obviously, you'll want to have appropriate plates, bowls, glasses, and flatware when it comes time to serve dinner. Up to this point, I've assumed you are not eating off the floor like a Caveman. You don't need to go out immediately and stock your kitchen with everything listed here. You can acquire this stuff over time. Be resourceful and check out yard sales, flea markets, or online outlets that offer these items at great deals. Meanwhile, improvise and make the most with what you have.

HARDWARE – Pots/Pans/Baking Dishes

12 inch Cast Iron Skillet with Lid - cast iron cookware is inexpensive and will last a lifetime. On top of that, it cooks evenly, retains heat, and is also believed to keep you healthy by supplying a steady dose of iron to your diet.

Grill Pan - a fantastic substitute for a grill. I prefer cast iron grill pans over the non-stick versions.

12 inch Non-Stick Skillet with Lid - the non-stick surface makes cleanup quick and easy.

Dutch Oven Style Pot with Lid - enameled cast iron is the best option; however any pot with a heavy bottom will do the trick. Great for making soups and braising meats.

1 Large 6-qt Pot with Lid - perfect for boiling pasta or potatoes.

1 Small 2.5-qt Pot with Lid - terrific for making sauces, steaming veggies, or heating liquids.

9x13 Pyrex Baking Dish - a must have for baking or roasting.

Non-Stick Baking Sheet - super cheap, and probably one of my most utilized items in the kitchen.

TOOLS AND ACCESSORIES

8 inch Chef's Knife with a Sharpening Steel - a chef's best friend. Don't go cheap here.

Cutting Board - I prefer a large wood cutting board over any other surface. Make sure it has a solid footing, so as not to slide while cutting.

Digital Meat Thermometer - a useful tool to make sure your meat is always perfectly cooked.

Potato Ricer/Masher - a ricer is a great tool for making silky smooth mashed potatoes. A masher is an even cheaper and more versatile tool that will provide a more rustic consistency.

Wine Opener - I prefer the ones that also have a bottle opener. A drill, drywall screw, and pliers will do the trick if you find yourself in a bind. Trust me.

Can Opener - get one that will fit her hands as well, as you may enlist her help in this area.

Peppermill - indispensable for any kitchen. Fresh Cracked pepper is worth the extra effort, and this tool makes it easy to always have fresh pepper on hand.

Box Cheese Grater - I like these because it provides several different options in one; a slicer, a rough grate, a fine grate, and an extra fine grate for harder cheeses. Choose one with a large bottom base to provide more stability.

Vegetable Peeler - fantastic for peeling vegetables or shaving cheeses.

Food Processor/Blender - the workhorse of the kitchen. Great for saving time and creating specialized dishes.

Colander - a must have for draining, washing, straining, or rinsing.

Wooden Spoon - heatproof and durable, I like having these in several different sizes.

Whisks - extremely versatile; fantastic for making vinaigrettes, dressings, or even a roux.

Spatula - I prefer stainless steel slotted spatulas.

Tongs - great for when you need a more precise touch.

Pot Holder/Oven Mitt - because I don't know anyone who likes to burn themselves. A folded towel will also work.

Measuring Cups and Spoons - these will be absolutely necessary to make sure you are getting the right measurements when following the recipes.

SERVING/STORAGE ITEMS

Assorted Mixing Bowls/Serving Bowls
Assorted Serving Plates or Platters
Plastic Storage Containers
Large Ziploc® Storage Bags
Aluminum Foil
Plastic Wrap
Wax/Parchment Paper

A Few Kitchen Pointers

◇ **USE FRESH INGREDIENTS** whenever possible. Your meal will only be as good as your ingredients.

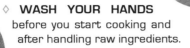

◇ **WASH YOUR HANDS** before you start cooking and after handling raw ingredients.

◇ You can speed up the ripening process of most fruit (especially avocados) by placing them in a closed brown paper grocery bag for several hours, up to a day or so.

◇ Try to avoid putting tomatoes in the fridge. The refrigerator affects the beneficial health components in the vegetable, and beyond that, taste. If you must, the fridge can add a few days of shelf life when necessary.

◇ Before cutting and juicing, place your lemons/limes in the microwave for 10-15 seconds, or roll them with your palm on a flat surface to get the most juice out of the fruit. Use a box or micro-plane grater to lightly zest (remove the outer skin) of the fruit. Be extra careful to only use the outer layer, as the inner white membrane tends to be bitter in flavor.

◇ Tastes and preferences vary widely. For that reason, several of these recipes will not include exact amounts of salt and pepper when seasoning dishes. It is important to taste throughout the cooking process and adjust seasoning when necessary. If you over season a dish, acidity (citrus, vinegar) works well, to a certain degree, to help cut the salty flavor.

◇ The **LOCAL VEGETABLE STAND** or **FARMERS MARKET** is a great place to shop for fruits, vegetables, and other artisan products. Items picked locally and right off the vine will always beat something that's been left to ripen in an 18-wheeler traveling across the country. Apart from being better in quality, locally grown ingredients are usually much cheaper because they aren't marked up to cover the cost of transportation.

◇ Get to know the folks who work at your local markets. The produce manager, butcher, and fishmonger will know what's fresh, and they are usually always willing to provide you with good information. If you are unsure, ask them to pick out fruits and vegetables that are ripe, or meats that look the best. Use their selection to help guide you when making future purchases. Whenever possible, have them trim your meats or devein/clean seafood to save time.

◇ Salads can be prepared in advance and kept fresh by covering with plastic wrap and keeping in the refrigerator while you complete the rest of the meal. To avoid soggy or wilted greens, wait to season or add the dressing until just before serving.

◇ If you don't have access to a grill, invest in a cast iron grill pan. The pan can be used over high heat on the stovetop to create those perfect grill marks, and it can go right into a high heated oven to allow those thicker cuts to cook through without burning.

◇ **DON'T OVER-THINK DESSERTS.** I don't expect, nor do I really want you to start baking cakes and pies. Ice cream, store-bought cookies or cakes, chocolate, fruits, cheeses, etc. are always appropriate and simple.

◇ Never put a piece of cast iron cookware in the dishwasher. Always wash or rinse the skillet with warm water and mild soap when necessary.

◇ Invest in some plastic storage containers. The recipes on the following pages will almost always yield leftovers. Take a few moments to save and put the leftovers away for lunch or dinner later on in the week.

IF ALL ELSE FAILS, ALWAYS HAVE A FEW BOTTLES OF GOOD RED WINE ON HAND AND THE NUMBER OF THAT GREAT ITALIAN TAKEOUT ON STANDBY. It's amazing how a few glasses of red wine can salvage any situation.

The Date

THINK SIMPLE.

BE PREPARED: read over the entire recipe and process before you get started. Shop, prep, or clean a few days or hours in advance. I have taken great care to describe the state or condition of all ingredients (minced, diced, chopped, etc) to assist you in advance of following each recipe. Make it easy on yourself and have all of the items prepped accordingly before beginning each recipe. Depending on the girl, it may be a good idea to ask beforehand if she's not particularly fond of certain food items so that you can plan ahead. Beware though, the more items on her list increases the odds that she's probably crazy. In all seriousness, you probably don't want to spend your date in the ER because you failed to ask her about any food allergies.

SET THE MOOD. Don't try too hard ... but try. Wear something nice but also comfortable, as you will be *working* in the kitchen. Give her a compliment and offer her a drink while you finish things up, tell her about the music that's playing, and maybe even set out an appetizer. Let her see that you are actually putting forth some *effort* in the kitchen. Use common sense about music. I'm not here to be your DJ, but at the same time I don't recommend making death metal the soundtrack to any of these meals. Everyone has his own preferences, so let her learn more about your personality by choosing tracks that you think are suitable for the evening. Don't forget about lighting. Remember that *Seinfeld* episode where Jerry was dating the "two-face"? You don't have to be a fan of the show to know that sometimes people look more or less attractive based on conditions, such as lighting. (Make sure you get her in direct light, at least once, so you know what you are working with). Rely on some subtler lighting choices and even some candles to help illuminate the evening. Girls tend to notice the small things; the candles are worth the extra effort.

KEEP IT CLEAN. Tidy up your place, clean the bathroom, empty the trash, and put away the dishes before you start cooking. Clean while you cook; wash or put away used bowls, pots, or utensils while you are waiting on other items to finish cooking. You don't want it to look like a hurricane came through the kitchen when you are ready to serve. I'll let you be the judge on doing the dishes after dinner. If she's the right kind of girl, it might be fun and to your advantage to roll up your sleeves and do some clean up together (she's a keeper). If she's an uptown girl, save the dishes for the next day (have fun with her, but get out while you still can).

BRUSH YOUR TEETH/Use mouthwash/Chew gum after dinner. These meals usually incorporate garlic in some form or another. Leave the wonderful flavors of dinner at dinner.

ABOVE ALL, BE YOURSELF. This book can't tell you what will win her heart in the end. I'm simply trying to provide you with instructions to create an experience. I could give you specific music to play, wines to drink, or topics for conversation, but at the end of the day you will come off looking like that dude that relies on snobby, expensive restaurants to impress women (insert: *The Beatles* "Can't Buy Me Love"). Be humble, have fun, and above all, always act like a gentleman. Trust me, you will be rewarded.

Pairing Food with Wine or Beer

P

AIRING A GREAT BEVERAGE WITH DINNER CAN OFTEN MAKE THE DIFFERENCE BETWEEN A GREAT MEAL AND ONE THAT IS EXCEPTIONAL.

It's important to always have a well balanced drink to accompany your hard work in the kitchen, not to mention the fact that alcohol can help take the edge off. Obviously there are thousands of books written on this subject, but my advice, like always, is to keep it simple. You don't have to spend a fortune to get a quality product. Talk to the staff at your local wine shop and ask for suggestions.

As you try new wines, take notes of what you did and did not like about each wine and use that as a guide for future purchases. In my experience, giving you a specific name or recommendation is usually pointless: A) It may not be stocked everywhere. B) You'll sound like a jackass trying to pronounce it at the store. C) You probably won't pay attention to my recommendation anyways. That being said, I do have some guidance for you. Red wines need to be served just below room temperature (Refrigerate for 10-15 minutes before serving), and white wines need to be served chilled (Refrigerate for at least an hour or more). As a general rule, lighter foods go with lighter wines (Whites) or beers (Lagers). Heavier foods go with heavier wines (Reds) and beers (Ales). Yes, there are some exceptions to the rule, so don't be afraid to get creative. Above all, trust your palate.

WINE/BEER

Sauvignon Blanc/Lagers
white or light fish, mild cheese, fruit

Chardonnay/Pilsners/Lagers/Cream Ales
grilled chicken, salmon, shellfish, and grilled fish;
anything with a scampi or cream sauce

Pinot Noir/Wheat Beers/Brown Ales
grilled fish, vegetables, or lighter meats - chicken,
pork, veal; pasta with cream or red sauce

Merlot/Pale Ales
red sauce pastas, red meat, sharp cheeses,
smoked or grilled foods

Zinfandel/Brown Ales
tomato pasta dishes, pizza, pesto, red meats,
chicken, heavier sauces

Cabernet Sauvignon/Porters/Stouts/Pale Ales
red meats, especially steak, grilled and
smoked foods

Syrah/Pale Ales/IPA's/Full Bodied Lagers
red meats, spicy foods, pan seared or
blackened fish

Rosé/Hefeweizen
salads, pasta salads, chicken, fish, light spicy foods

The Weeknight Date

I realize that most of you are new to this. These are the easiest recipes and pairings in the book. For the more experienced, these can be used when time is short, or when you are looking for an everyday meal that can be made without too much hassle. Remember, you don't have to make everything listed on a menu. In this case, I've given you either a salad or an appetizer to go along with the entrée; however the entrée alone will always be sufficient. You decide how much time you have and what you want to serve. I'm here to give you options and direction.

Spicy Arugula and Pancetta Salad

Pancetta is basically the Italian form of bacon. You should be able to find this item at the deli counter in most grocery stores. Have them slice it thin, but don't accept their invitation to try a sample. Of course, if you can't find the pancetta, bacon will always be an appropriate substitute. Green onions can also be substituted for the chives.

4 Slices Pancetta, thinly sliced
1 ½ Tablespoons Red Wine Vinegar*
¼ Cup Extra Virgin Olive Oil*
1 Pinch Kosher Salt*
¼ Teaspoon Fresh Cracked Pepper*
4 Cups Pre-Washed Arugula, loosely packed
2 Teaspoons Chives, finely chopped

Heat a cast iron skillet over medium heat. Add pancetta and cook until crispy and fat has rendered, turning once, 5-6 minutes. Remove pancetta from heat and place on paper towels to drain excess fat and cool. In a separate mixing bowl, add vinegar, olive oil, salt, and pepper and whisk until incorporated. In a serving bowl, toss dressing with arugula and chives. Garnish with pancetta, gently broken by hand into bite size pieces.

Italian Sausage, Portobello's, and Spinach over Penne a la Vodka

This hearty dish is one of the quintessential recipes of this book; simple, affordable, and satisfying. Pairs well with Chianti, Pinot Noir, Merlot, or Amber Ale.

1 Teaspoon Kosher Salt*
8 oz Dry Penne Pasta
½ lb Mild Italian Sausage
8 oz Sliced Portobello Mushrooms
3 Cups Fresh Spinach Leaves, loosely packed
1 Jar Classico® Brand Vodka Sauce
(Spaghetti sauce aisle)
Parmigiano Reggiano Cheese, grated

Heat a large pot of water with 1 teaspoon of kosher salt over high heat. Add pasta and boil for 11-12 minutes, or al dente; drain and set aside. Meanwhile, remove the outer casings from the sausage and add to a cast iron skillet over medium heat. As the sausage begins to brown, add the mushrooms and continue to cook until the sausage is completely browned and cooked through, 10-12 minutes. Add the spinach leaves and cook 2-3 minutes until the leaves have wilted down and blended with the other ingredients. Add the Vodka sauce and heat to a simmer, 4-5 minutes. Add drained penne pasta to the meat/sauce mixture and toss to incorporate. Serve. Garnish with fresh grated cheese to taste.

Spring Mix Salad

The lemon juice will add a nice splash of citrus to help freshen up the bitterness in the mixed greens. The spring mix salad blend can be found in the produce section of most stores, along with the other bagged greens.

4 Cups Pre-Washed Spring Mix Salad, loosely packed
6 Cherry Tomatoes, halved
¼ Small Red Onion, thinly sliced
¼ Cup Extra Virgin Olive Oil*
½ Large Lemon, juiced*
¼ Teaspoon Kosher Salt*
¼ Teaspoon Fresh Cracked Pepper*
2 oz Shaved Parmigiano Reggiano Cheese

Combine greens, tomatoes, and red onion into a large serving bowl. In a separate mixing bowl, combine oil and lemon juice and whisk vigorously to combine. Pour the mixture over the salad and season with salt and pepper, toss. Using a chef's knife or vegetable peeler, shave the Parmigiano Reggiano into shards. Top the salad with cheese and serve.

Sautéed Chicken with Asparagus, Portobello's, and Tomatoes over Spaghetti

This versatile dish works just as well during the summer as it does during the winter. Satisfying, yet light and fresh, this dish pairs well with Pinot Noir, Chardonnay, or Lager.

8 oz Dry Spaghetti Pasta
2 6-8 oz Chicken Breasts, pounded thin
Kosher Salt*
Fresh Cracked Pepper*
3 Tablespoons Extra Virgin Olive Oil*
½ Cup Dry White Wine
2 Garlic Cloves, thinly sliced*
8 oz Sliced Portobello Mushrooms
½ lb Fresh Asparagus, cleaned, trimmed, and sliced in half
1 14.5 oz Can Petite Diced Tomatoes
½ Cup Chicken Broth
Parmigiano Reggiano Cheese, grated

Heat a large pot of salted water over high heat. Add pasta and boil for 9-10 minutes, or al dente; drain and set aside. Meanwhile, heat a cast iron skillet over medium high heat and season chicken breasts with salt and pepper. Add oil, followed by the chicken to the skillet and cook, turning once, until internal temperature reaches 160 degrees F, about 7-9 minutes. Transfer chicken to a plate and tent with foil to keep warm. Deglaze skillet with wine and add garlic and mushrooms; cook until mushrooms begin to soften, 3-4 minutes. Add asparagus, tomatoes, and chicken broth, cook for another 4-5 minutes. Pour cooked pasta into the skillet with the other ingredients and toss thoroughly, remove from heat. Slice chicken on the bias. Plate pasta and vegetables and top with sliced chicken. Serve. Garnish with fresh grated cheese to taste.

Tex's Loaded Queso

Inspired from a friend "Tex," a native of Austin, TX. Like anything from Texas, this is bigger and better than any other cheese dip you've ever had, or at least those Texans think so. Check with your local specialty food stores or Mexican grocers to find the fresh ground chorizo sausage. Keep the cheese sauce and the chorizo/beans mixture separated until just before serving.

½ lb Fresh Ground Chorizo Sausage, casings removed
½ Jalapeño, seeded and finely diced
1 15 oz Can Black Beans, drained
½ lb White American Cheese, grated or sliced thin (Deli section)
5 oz Half and Half
1 Avocado, diced
Tortilla Chips

In a cast iron skillet over medium heat, add chorizo and jalapeño and cook until the sausage is browned, 6-8 minutes, drain excess fat and grease (a paper towel can be used to blot extra grease if necessary). Reduce heat to medium-low; add black beans, heat through, stirring on occasion. Meanwhile, in a separate pot over medium-low heat, add half-and-half and cheese. Continue to stir constantly and keep a close watch as the cheese melts, careful not to burn; mixture should be fully melted and smooth without lumps. In a large serving bowl, scoop a large portion of the chorizo and bean mixture into the bottom of the serving bowl. Next, pour a generous serving of the cheese mixture over the top of the chorizo and beans, enough to just cover. Top with diced avocado and serve immediately with warmed tortilla chips.

Seared Grouper with Mango Salsa and Black Beans

Mangos add just the right amount of citrus to accompany the saltiness of the seared fish. Mangos are best purchased when in season, from late spring to early fall. The cool sour cream will offset the heat from the jalapeño. Serve with a Mexican beer (Bohemia®, Dos Equis Amber®, Corona®) or a Red Spanish Rioja wine.

1 Cup Mango, diced
½ Jalapeño, seeded and finely diced
¼ Cup Canned Roasted Red Peppers, drained and diced
1 Lime, juiced
1 15 oz Can Black Beans in seasoned sauce
2 Tablespoons Extra Virgin Olive Oil*
2 6-8 oz Grouper Filets
½ Teaspoon Cajun Seasoning*
2 Tablespoons Sour Cream
1 Tablespoon Red Onion, finely diced

In a small bowl, combine mango, jalapeño, roasted peppers, and lime juice; mix and set aside. In a small pot, heat beans over medium low heat until they begin to simmer, 8-10 minutes. Meanwhile, preheat a cast iron skillet over medium high heat, add oil. Season both sides of the grouper filets with Cajun seasoning. Add filets to the skillet and cook undisturbed, turning once, for 3-4 minutes per side, or until fish reaches 140 degrees F internal temperature. Remove grouper and beans from heat, and plate side by side. Top the grouper with a tablespoon of the mango salsa. Top the black beans with a tablespoon of sour cream, followed by a sprinkle of red onions. Serve immediately.

Bruschetta

You'll find several variations of this classic in almost every cookbook. The salty and tangy feta in this version pairs well with the sweet basil and tomato.

½ Loaf French Bread, cut into ½ inch slices
¼ Cup Extra Virgin Olive Oil, reserves for garnish*
Fresh Cracked Pepper*
2 Roma Tomatoes, thinly sliced
4 oz Crumbled Feta Cheese
6-8 Fresh Basil Leaves*

Preheat oven to 400 degrees F. Lay out bread slices on a baking sheet and brush generously with olive oil and season with fresh cracked pepper. Place pan in the oven and bake 6-8 minutes, or until edges are golden brown. Immediately top with a slice of tomato and crumbled feta and return to oven for 2-3 minutes. Meanwhile carefully stack and roll the basil leaves together and thinly slice, or chiffonade. Remove bruschetta from oven and garnish with fresh basil and a light drizzle of remaining olive oil over the top of each slice. Serve.

Chicken Tenderloins with White Beans, Spinach, and Roasted Tomatoes

Savory and rustic; this stew like meal is perfect for a fall or winter evening. Pair with Pinot Noir, Chardonnay, Sauvignon Blanc, or a lighter Lager/Pilsner.

1 Pint Cherry Tomatoes
4 Tablespoons Extra Virgin Olive Oil, divided*
Kosher Salt*
Fresh Cracked Pepper*
4 Cloves Garlic, crushed and peeled*
1 lb (6-8) Chicken Tenderloins
1 Cup Dry White Wine or Chicken Broth
3 Cups Fresh Spinach Leaves, loosely packed
1 15 oz Can Cannellini Beans, or Great Northern/ Navy Beans, drained
2 oz Shaved Parmigiano Reggiano Cheese

Preheat oven to 400 degrees F. On a baking sheet, drizzle tomatoes with 2 tablespoons of olive oil and season with salt and pepper. Place garlic cloves in each corner of the baking sheet and roast in the oven, uncovered, 20-25 minutes, or until tomatoes are just beginning to burst. Meanwhile, in a cast iron skillet over medium high heat, add remaining oil and season chicken tenderloins with salt and pepper. Add tenderloins to the skillet and brown on two sides, about 2-3 minutes per side. Next, deglaze the skillet with white wine or chicken broth. Add spinach and stir until leaves have wilted. Next, add beans and heat through, 4-5 minutes. Remove skillet from heat and plate mixture in bowls, topping each with equal portions of chicken tenderloins. Remove tomatoes from oven and carefully arrange around the plate, discard the garlic. Garnish with shaved Parmigiano Reggiano cheese. Serve.

Bistro Salad

The buttery flavor of the Bibb lettuce is matched by the creamy texture of the Italian dressing in this quick salad. The presentation of this dish lends itself well to being made in advance and kept in the fridge until ready to dress and serve.

1 Small Head Bibb lettuce, halved, core removed
4 Cherry Tomatoes, halved
¼ Small Red Onion, finely diced
Newman's Own® Creamy Italian Dressing
2 Basil Leaves, for garnish*

Arrange the lettuce halves, core side up on two serving plates. Carefully arrange the tomato and onion slices inside of the hollowed out core on top of each salad. Drizzle the dressing on top of the salad. Top each plate with a fresh basil leaf to garnish.

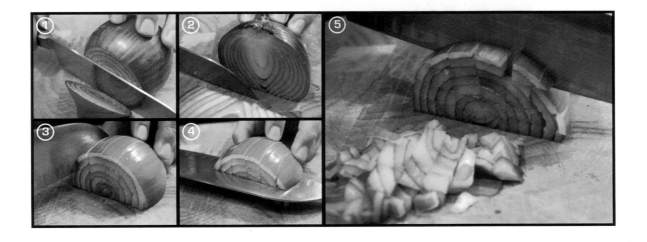

Shrimp and Sea Scallop Scampi

The shrimp and scallops are the standout in this dish, so be sure to splurge on fresh ingredients. This scampi sauce is a simplified version of a seafood staple. Pair with Chardonnays with high oak concentrations or a cold Stella Artois®.

8 oz Dry Linguine Pasta
1 Teaspoon Kosher Salt*
3 Tablespoons Butter, 1 tablespoon reserved*
2 Tablespoons Extra Virgin Olive Oil*
½ lb Large Pink Shrimp, peeled and deveined with the tail on
½ lb Large Sea Scallops
½ Teaspoon Cajun Seasoning*
½ Lemon*
1 Small Shallot, minced
2 Cloves Garlic, minced*
1 Cup Dry White Wine or Chicken Broth
1 14.5 oz Can Petite Diced Tomatoes
3-4 Sprigs Fresh Flat Leaf Parsley, finely chopped*

Heat a large pot of water with 1 teaspoon of kosher salt over high heat and bring to a boil. Add pasta and cook for 7-8 minutes, or just under al dente. Drain the pasta and set aside. In the meantime, melt 2 tablespoons of butter into 2 tablespoons of olive oil over medium high heat in a skillet. Season shrimp and scallops with Cajun seasoning and add to skillet. Cook for 2-3 minutes until shrimp are just pink and scallops are beginning to firm; remove from pan and place on a plate to keep warm, squeezing the juice of ½ lemon over the top. Add shallots and garlic to the empty pan and cook for 1-2 minutes, or until shallots start to become translucent. Deglaze the skillet with the wine (or broth). Add the petite diced tomatoes and bring to a slow simmer, 2-3 minutes. Finally, add the shrimp, scallops, and pasta into the pan and heat through, 2-3 minutes. Remove from heat and add the last tablespoon of butter, stir until completely incorporated. Toss and serve immediately. Garnish with parsley.

Roasted Garlic Bread

Roasting garlic takes some time, but it couldn't be easier. The flavor and aromas it creates in the kitchen will definitely be worth the extra time and effort. Roasted garlic can always be prepared a few days in advance and kept refrigerated in an airtight container until ready for use.

½ Head Garlic*
2 Tablespoons Extra Virgin Olive Oil*
Fresh Cracked Pepper*
½ Loaf French Bread
1 Teaspoon Dried Oregano*
½ Stick Unsalted Butter, at room temperature*

Preheat oven to 400 degrees F. Place garlic head on a sheet of aluminum foil and drizzle with olive oil and fresh cracked pepper. Carefully seal the garlic with the foil and roast in the oven for 20-25 minutes. Remove garlic from oven and set aside to cool. Meanwhile, make diagonal slices on the bread every inch or so, careful not to slice all the way through the bottom of the loaf. Remove garlic from the foil and squeeze the roasted cloves from the skin, yielding about 1-2 tablespoons of roasted garlic. In a small bowl, mix the roasted garlic and dried oregano with the unsalted butter using a fork to incorporate the ingredients, making a compound butter. Generously spread the compound butter on the inside and outside of the sliced bread and bake on a baking sheet for 7-8 minutes at 400 degrees F. Serve.

Chicken Parmesan

Another traditional favorite, lightened up a bit by avoiding an egg wash to form the crust. The secret to making this dish perfectly is pounding out the chicken to make it extra tender. Serve with Chianti, Zinfandel, Pinot Noir, or Merlot.

1 lb Boneless Skinless Chicken Breast, pounded thin and cut into 2 inch strips
½ Cup Extra Virgin Olive Oil, divided*
Kosher Salt*
Fresh Cracked Pepper*
1 Cup Seasoned Italian Bread Crumbs
½ Cup Parmigiano Reggiano Cheese, grated
1 Jar Classico® Tomato and Basil Spaghetti Sauce
8 oz Shredded Mozzarella Cheese
8 oz Dry Thin Spaghetti Pasta

Preheat oven to 350 degrees F. Drizzle chicken strips with ¼ cup of olive oil and season with salt and pepper. On a separate plate, combine bread crumbs and Parmigiano Reggiano cheese. Dredge each chicken strip into the breadcrumb mixture, ensuring an even coat. Heat a cast iron skillet over medium heat, add remaining ¼ cup of oil. Add the strips (3-4 at a time), and pan fry, turning once until internal temperature reaches 160 degrees F, about 3-4 minutes each side; repeat in batches until all strips have been cooked. Place cooked strips into a 9x13 glass baking dish and top with tomato sauce. Top sauce with shredded mozzarella cheese and bake in oven for 20-25 minutes, until cheese is bubbly and slightly browned. Meanwhile, heat a large pot of salted water over high heat and cook spaghetti until al dente, 9-10 minutes; drain and set aside. Remove chicken from oven and allow it to rest for 5 minutes. Plate spaghetti and top with chicken and sauce. Serve immediately.

Mediterranean Salsa

Light, easy, and big on flavor. This salsa keeps fresh in a refrigerated airtight container up to one day in advance. If not serving immediately, avoid adding the avocado until just before serving.

2 Roma Tomatoes, seeded and diced
¼ Small Red Onion, diced
½ Cucumber, diced
1 Avocado, diced
4 oz Crumbled Feta
¼ Cup Extra Virgin Olive Oil*
2 Tablespoons Red Wine Vinegar*
1 Teaspoon Dried Oregano*
¼ Teaspoon Kosher Salt*
¼ Teaspoon Fresh Cracked Pepper*
Pita Chips for serving

Combine first five ingredients into a large serving bowl. In a separate mixing bowl, combine oil, vinegar, and oregano and whisk vigorously to combine ingredients. Pour the mixture over the vegetables and cheese. Season with salt and pepper, toss, and allow the salsa to sit and marinate a few minutes before serving. Serve with pita chips.

Grilled Pizza Margarita

Why bake when you can grill? Most chain grocery stores sell refrigerated dough in the bakery section. If you don't have an outdoor grill, this recipe can also work inside the kitchen. Use a grill pan to create a nice sear on the crust, and finish it off by adding the other ingredients and placing the pizza directly on the top rack of an oven heated to 400 degrees F. The grilled crust stands up well to the hearty toppings. Pair with Zinfandel, Pinot Noir, or a cold Budweiser®.

16 oz Frozen or Refrigerated Pizza Dough
¼ Cup Extra Virgin Olive oil*
¼ Teaspoon Red Pepper Flakes, divided*
1 Cup Canned Chopped Tomatoes, in heavy puree, divided
8 oz Fresh Mozzarella Cheese, thinly sliced
6-8 Cherry Tomatoes, cut in half, divided
10-12 Fresh Basil Leaves*

Follow instructions on dough package to all allow sufficient time for the dough to rise if needed. Drizzle the olive oil on a non stick baking sheet. Using a sharp knife, cut the dough ball in half and roll each half in the oil to coat. Using your hands, roughly work the dough into two equal shapes of your preference, about 8-10 inches in diameter and ¼ inch thick. Make sure the thickness is consistent throughout. Heat one side of the grill to medium high, if using charcoal place coals on one side only. Using a paper towel dipped in olive oil, quickly brush the entire grill grate to create a non-stick surface. Carefully place each portion directly over the hot surface of the grill, catching any edges using tongs. After roughly 1 minute, the top of the dough will become puffy and the underside will stiffen, leaving nice grill marks. Immediately flip each portion using tongs and place on the cool side of the grill. Brush each portion with olive oil and sprinkle with red pepper flakes. Spread an even layer of the pureed tomatoes on top of each portion, leaving the edges clean to create a crust. Next, top evenly with cheese and tomatoes. Move dough back towards heat, but not completely over direct heat. Using tongs, continue to rotate each pizza every 45-60 seconds, careful not to burn, to ensure each section receives high heat. Continue for 6-8 minutes covering the grill from time to time, until the top is bubbly and the cheese has melted. Top evenly with roughly chopped basil and any remaining olive oil. Cut each pizza into quarters and serve immediately.

Stuffed Mushrooms

These mushrooms are hearty in flavor and work great as a finger food. The stuffing can be made up to 1 day in advance and kept covered in the refrigerator. Try buying the biggest button mushrooms available to make it easier when removing the stems and adding the stuffing.

½ **Cup Italian Style Breadcrumbs**
½ **Cup Parmigiano Reggiano Cheese, grated**
1 **Clove Garlic, finely minced** *
½ **Lemon, juiced** *
¼ **Cup Extra Virgin Olive Oil** *
8 **oz Large Button Mushrooms, stems removed**
Kosher Salt *
Fresh Cracked Pepper *

Preheat oven to 400 degrees F. In a small mixing bowl, combine breadcrumbs, cheese, garlic, lemon juice, and olive oil. Toss mixture to blend. Using a spoon, carefully dig out the area of the mushroom where the stems were removed to create a cavity for the stuffing. On a baking sheet, lay out the mushroom caps and season with kosher salt and fresh cracked pepper. Using a spoon, fill each cavity with the stuffing. Bake the mushrooms until tender and filling is browned on top; 15-20 minutes. Serve.

Pasta Mediterranean

A great dish for that one vegetarian girl you convinced yourself into having over for dinner. Pair with Pinot Noir, Chardonnay, Lager, or a Soy-Milk cocktail.

¼ Cup Extra Virgin Olive Oil*
2 Garlic Cloves, minced*
¼ Teaspoon Red Pepper Flakes*
1 Cup Cherry Tomatoes
½ Cup Canned Artichoke Hearts in water, drained and quartered
3 Cups Fresh Spinach Leaves, loosely packed
¼ Cup Kalamata Olives, pitted
½ Cup Chicken Broth
Kosher Salt*
Fresh Cracked Pepper*
8 oz Farfalle (Bow Tie) Pasta
4 oz Feta Cheese, crumbled

Preheat a large pot of salted water over high heat. Meanwhile, add oil to a preheated cast iron skillet over medium heat. Add garlic and red pepper flakes and cook for 30-45 seconds, careful not to brown garlic. Add tomatoes, artichokes, spinach, and olives and cook 4-5 minutes until the spinach has wilted. Next, add chicken broth, and season with salt and pepper. Add pasta to the boiling water and cook 11-12 minutes, or al dente. Before draining pasta, add about ½ cup of the pasta water into the skillet with the other ingredients. Drain pasta; add into the skillet and toss to combine with the other ingredients. Top with crumbled feta. Serve.

Goat Cheese and Spinach Salad

Crunchy, sweet, and tangy. The perfect accompaniment to a savory grilled pork chop. Try a Rosé wine or a Hefewiezen beer with this salad.

4 Cups Pre-Washed Spinach, loosely packed
½ Green (Granny Smith) Apple, diced into bite size pieces
¼ Small Red Onion, thinly sliced
2 Tablespoons Pecans, halved
¼ Cup Extra Virgin Olive Oil*
1 ½ Tablespoons Balsamic Vinegar*
¼ Teaspoon Kosher Salt*
¼ Teaspoon Fresh Cracked Pepper*
¼ Cup Crumbled Goat Cheese

Combine the first four ingredients into a large serving bowl. In a mixing bowl, combine oil and vinegar and whisk vigorously until combined. Drizzle the dressing over the greens and season with salt and pepper. Toss to coat the leaves evenly. Top with goat cheese and serve.

Grilled Bone-In Pork Chops with Roasted Vegetables

The Herbs de Provence seasoning will add a clean, organic flavor to the roasted vegetables. You can find this seasoning blend in the spice section of most high end grocery stores. Italian blend seasonings are also readily available and can be used as a substitute for the Herbs de Provence. Pairs well with either Pinot Noir or Amber ale.

¾ Cup Extra Virgin Olive Oil*
¼ Cup Soy Sauce*
2 Cloves Garlic, minced*
2 8-10 oz Bone-In Pork Chops
1 Large Zucchini, roughly chopped
1 Large Yellow Squash, roughly chopped
1 Large Red Onion, roughly chopped
1 Large Red Bell Pepper, roughly chopped

Kosher Salt*
Fresh Cracked Pepper*
2 Teaspoons Herbs de Provence Seasoning*

At least one hour before grilling, add ½ cup of oil, soy sauce, and garlic into a large Ziploc® bag. Season chops lightly with salt and pepper and add to bag. Marinate up to one day in advance, keeping in refrigerator. Heat grill over medium high. Preheat oven to 400 degrees F. Add vegetables into a large glass baking dish and drizzle with the remaining ¼ cup of oil and season with salt, pepper, and Herbs de Provence seasoning. Roast vegetables until slightly browned and fork tender, about 20-25 minutes. Add chops to grill, cover, and cook undisturbed, turning once, until internal temperature reaches 150 degrees F, or 12-15 minutes depending on the size and cut. Remove chops and allow to rest 3-4 minutes before serving. Plate the vegetables in the center of the plate, while resting the pork chop on top. Serve immediately.

Roasted Garlic Creole Bread

If you are short on time, skip the roasted garlic and mix in a ¼ teaspoon of garlic powder to the compound butter. Serve on the side of the gumbo for dipping.

½ Head Garlic*
2 Tablespoons Extra Virgin Olive Oil*
Fresh Cracked Pepper*
½ Loaf French Bread
¼ Teaspoon Cajun Seasoning*
½ Stick Unsalted Butter, at room temperature*

Preheat oven to 400 degrees F. Place garlic head on a sheet of aluminum foil and drizzle with olive oil and fresh cracked pepper. Carefully seal the garlic with the foil and roast in the oven for 20-25 minutes. Remove garlic from oven and set aside to cool. Meanwhile, make diagonal slices on the bread every inch or so, careful not to slice all the way through the bottom of the loaf. Remove garlic from the foil and squeeze the roasted cloves from the skin, yielding about 1-2 tablespoons of roasted garlic. In a small bowl, mix the roasted garlic and Cajun seasoning with the unsalted butter using a fork to incorporate the ingredients, making a compound butter. Generously spread the compound butter on the inside and outside of the sliced bread and bake on a baking sheet for 7-8 minutes at 400 degrees F. Serve.

Shrimp Gumbo

This dish screams comfort food. It's absolutely perfect for a fall or winter evening date at home. Spend the extra time to carefully make the roux, slowly. If the roux burns ... start over. Cooked Andouille sausage or chicken is a great substitute for the shrimp when a heartier, more affordable version is desired. Pairs great with a crisp Chardonnay, Pinot Grigio, or Abita Amber Ale®.

¼ Cup Vegetable Oil
¼ Cup All Purpose Flour
1 Medium Yellow Onion, finely diced
1 Green Bell Pepper, finely diced
3 Cloves Garlic, finely minced*
1 Tablespoon Cajun Seasoning*
32 oz Chicken Broth
16 oz Frozen Cut Okra
2 lbs Large Shrimp, peeled and deveined
2 Teaspoons Green Onions, finely sliced for garnish
Hot Cooked Rice, to serve

In a Dutch oven or large heavy bottomed pot, heat oil and flour together over medium heat, whisking constantly to create a dark roux (about the color of a dull penny), or about 12-14 minutes. Stir in onion and bell pepper, and cook 6-8 minutes, or until onions become tender and translucent. Add garlic and Cajun seasoning. In 1 cup intervals, slowly whisk in chicken broth until fully incorporated. Cover, and allow the mixture to come to a slow boil, 12-15 minutes. As mixture comes to a boil, add okra, cover, and simmer for another 10-12 minutes. Taste and adjust flavor by using Cajun Seasoning as necessary. Add shrimp, cover, and remove from heat. Allow the shrimp to cook for 5-6 minutes, until they are firm and bright pink. Serve immediately in large bowls topped with hot cooked rice. Garnish with Green Onions.

The Weekend Date

Lucky you ... The weekend date is definitely a step up, thus these recipes will take more time and patience. The same principles apply as always; keep things as fresh and as simple as possible. Perhaps you'll have more time on these days to create a few more of the items off the suggested menus. Again, all of the control is in your hands.

Guacamole

Keep it simple here. Quality, ripe avocados are the key to a great guacamole. Choose avocados that are soft yet still firm. If you're not sure, ask the attractive older lady who's also shopping in the produce section for some help.

2 Cloves Garlic, finely minced*
¼ Teaspoon Kosher Salt*
2 Ripe Hass Avocados, peeled and seed removed, diced into chunks
½ Medium Lemon, juiced*
Tortilla Chips, for serving

On a cutting board, combine the minced garlic and kosher salt. Using a chef's knife, work ingredients into a paste on the board. Combine garlic paste, avocados, and lemon juice into a small mixing bowl and mash with a fork until avocados have softened and incorporated all of the juice, taste and adjust seasoning if necessary. Mixture should be creamy with some large chunks of avocado remaining. Serve with tortilla chips.

Southwestern BBQ Ranch Salad

The mixture of the BBQ sauce with the ranch adds that kick of smoke and tang that makes this salad irresistible.

1 Heart of Romaine Lettuce, torn into bite sized pieces
½ Cup Pepper Jack Cheese, grated
¼ Cup Canned Corn, drained
¼ Cup Canned Black Beans, drained
1 Vine Ripe Tomato, finely diced
¼ Cup Cilantro, roughly chopped as garnish
Naturally Fresh® Ranch Dressing
BBQ Sauce, any vinegar based sauce is appropriate

Place lettuce in the bottom of a large serving bowl. Top salad with cheese, corn, black beans, tomatoes, and garnish with cilantro. In a separate mixing bowl, combine 3 parts ranch dressing to 1 part BBQ sauce. Serve with dressing on the side.

Southwestern Chicken with Black Beans and Yellow Rice

The colors of this dish are outstanding. Savory, simple, and affordable; this dish pairs well with a Mexican Beer (Corona®, Dos Equis®, Negro Modelo®), Spanish Red Wines (Riojas), or even a Margarita (on the rocks of course). Omit the chicken for a vegetarian friendly meal. That is, of course, assuming she made it back for round two.

1 5 oz Package Yellow Rice
2 Tablespoons Extra Virgin Olive Oil*
2 8 oz Chicken Breasts, pounded thin
1 Tablespoon Chili Powder
1 Teaspoon Garlic Powder*
Kosher Salt*
Fresh Cracked Pepper*
1 10 oz Can Original Rotel® Tomatoes
1 15 oz Can Black Beans
½ Cup Monterey Jack Cheese, grated
¼ Cup Black Olives, thinly sliced
2 Teaspoons Green Onions, garnish

Preheat oven to 300 degrees F. In a small pot, cook rice according to instructions on package. Heat a cast iron skillet over medium high heat and add oil. Season chicken breasts with chili powder, garlic powder, salt, and pepper; add to skillet. Cook, turning once, until internal temperature reaches 165 degrees F, about 8-10 minutes. Remove chicken from skillet and set aside on a plate, tent with foil to keep warm. Add the Rotel® tomatoes and black beans to the skillet and heat until warm, about 4-5 minutes. Start plating in layers; rice, bean and tomato mixture, and chicken. Finish by topping the entree with cheese, olives, and green onions. Add plated entrees to the warmed oven until cheese is melted. Serve, careful of hot plate.

Hummus with Toasted Pitas

A good tip is to warm the chickpeas in the micro-wave for 30 seconds or so before combining with the other ingredients. This will ensure that the hummus is extra smooth and creamy. Tahini is a sesame seed paste that can be found at most high-end grocers or specialty food stores. If you are short on time, this appetizer can be simpli-fied by serving the warmed pitas alongside your favorite brand of store bought hummus.

3-4 Pita Bread Circles, quartered
2 Garlic Cloves, minced*
1 Can Chick-Peas, drained and rinsed
¼ Cup Tahini
½ Lemon, juiced*
¼ Cup Extra Virgin Olive Oil, plus 1 Tablespoon for garnish*
¼ Cup Water
Paprika, as garnish

Preheat oven to 200 degrees F. Lay out quartered pita slices on a baking sheet and place into oven to warm 6-8 minutes. Meanwhile, combine the remain-ing ingredients, except for the paprika, into a food processor and blend until the mixture is smooth and well combined. Add more water, in tablespoon incre-ments, if a thinner consistency is desired. Remove from the food processor and place into a medium sized serving bowl. Leave a small indention in the middle of the paste and drizzle with 1 tablespoon of oil. Lightly dust the hummus with paprika and serve with warmed pitas. Hummus can be made 3 days in advance and kept covered in the refrigerator.

Greek Salad

This salad is an everyday staple in my family. The classic Greek inspired flavors and ingredients in this salad make for a great presentation. Top with grilled chicken, steak, or shrimp to create a meal on its own.

1 Heart of Romaine Lettuce, torn into bite sized pieces
½ Cucumber, cut into bite-sized pieces
¼ Medium Red Onion, thinly sliced
1 Vine Ripe Tomato, quartered
2 oz Pitted Kalamata Olives
4 oz Crumbled Feta Cheese
¾ Cup Extra Virgin Olive Oil*
¼ Cup Red Wine Vinegar*
1 Teaspoon Dried Oregano*
½ Teaspoon Kosher Salt*
½ Teaspoon Fresh Cracked Pepper*

Combine the first six ingredients into a large serving bowl. In a separate mixing bowl, combine oil, vinegar, and oregano and whisk vigorously to combine ingre-dients. Pour mixture over salad and cheese. Season with salt and pepper, toss, and allow the salad to sit and marinate a few minutes before serving.

Chicken Kabobs over Rice Pilaf

Kebabs change up the presentation and make the dining experience a bit more relaxed and hands on. Add a dash of cinnamon to the rice pilaf for an extra authentic Mediterranean flavor. Pair with Syrah or Brown Ales.

½ Cup Extra Virgin Olive Oil*
2 Tablespoons Red Wine Vinegar*
½ Lemon, juiced*
2 Cloves Garlic, minced*
1 lb Chicken Breast, cut into two inch cubes
1 Large Red Onion, cut into two inch pieces
1 Large Bell Pepper, cut into two inch pieces
Kosher Salt*
Fresh Cracked Pepper*
1 Teaspoon Dried Oregano*
8 (6 inch) Bamboo Skewers, soaked in water for 10 minutes
6 Tablespoons Unsalted butter*
1 Cup Converted Rice
½ Cup Vermicelli Pasta, crushed
3 Cups Chicken Broth

At least one hour before grilling, add oil, red wine vinegar, lemon juice, and garlic into a large Ziploc® bag. Season chicken, onions, and peppers liberally with salt, pepper, and oregano and add to bag. Marinate up to one day in advance, keeping in refrigerator. Heat grill over medium high. Begin assembling kebabs, ensuring an even distribution of chicken, onions, and peppers on each skewer, set aside. Melt the butter in a skillet over medium high heat, add rice and vermicelli, and stir every few minutes until the rice becomes opaque and the pasta begins to brown, 6-8 minutes. Slowly add the chicken broth and allow the ingredients to come to a boil. Cover, and reduce heat to low, simmering for 15-20 minutes, or until all the broth has been absorbed. Add kebabs to a covered grill and cook, turning every 3-4 minutes, until internal temperature reaches 165 degrees F, about 10-12 minutes. Remove rice from heat, fluff with fork, and plate. Remove kebabs from grill and rest on top of the rice pilaf. Serve.

Sautéed Shrimp

When zesting a lemon, always be sure to use the outer layer of the fruit only. Do not use any of the bitter white part of the skin. The oils from the zest will really shine through with the sweet flavor of the shrimp.

2 Tablespoons Extra Virgin Olive Oil*
1 Pinch Red Pepper Flakes*
1 lb Large Shrimp, peeled and deveined
1 Garlic Clove, minced*
½ Lemon, with ¼ teaspoon of minced zest*
1 Pinch Kosher Salt*
1 Tablespoon Unsalted Butter*
1 Tablespoon Fresh Parsley, finely chopped for garnish*

In a large non-stick skillet over medium-high heat, add oil and red pepper flakes; sauté for 30 seconds. Add shrimp, garlic, lemon zest, and salt; sauté for 2-3 minutes. Add the juice of ½ lemon and continue to sauté until shrimp are firm and bright pink, 1-2 minutes. Stir in and melt butter, remove from heat. Garnish with chopped parsley. Serve immediately.

Blue Cheese and Spinach Salad

A salad with great contrasts; crunchy almonds, sweet and chewy cranberries, and the salty bite of blue cheese. Gorgonzola is always a good substitute for the blue cheese.

4 Cups Pre-Washed Spinach Leaves, loosely packed
¼ Cup Dried Cranberries
2 Tablespoons Almonds, sliced

1 ½ Tablespoons Balsamic Vinegar*
¼ Cup Extra Virgin Olive Oil*
1 Pinch Kosher Salt*
¼ Cup Crumbled Blue Cheese

Combine first three ingredients into a large serving bowl. In a separate mixing bowl, whisk together vinegar, oil, and salt until incorporated. Drizzle dressing over greens and toss lightly until leaves are coated. Top with crumbled blue cheese. Serve.

Flat Iron Steak with Sautéed Spinach and Baked Potatoes

Flat Iron steak is a relatively new cut of meat that's known for being affordable, yet tender and big on flavor. This cut is best served when sliced thin on the bias as described in this recipe. Pairs well with Merlot, Cabernet, Amber, and Stout.

¼ Cup Extra Virgin Olive Oil*
2 Tablespoons Balsamic Vinegar*
2 Cloves Garlic, minced*
1 Large 12-16 oz Flat Iron Steak
Kosher Salt*
Fresh Cracked Pepper*
2 Large Baking Potatoes
1 ½ Tablespoons Unsalted Butter*
1 9 oz Bag Fresh Baby Spinach Leaves
Unsalted Butter (Potato Topping)
Sour Cream (Potato Topping)
2 Teaspoons Fresh Chives, finely chopped
(Potato Topping)

At least one hour before grilling, add oil, balsamic vinegar, and garlic into a large Ziploc® bag. Season steak liberally with salt and pepper and add to bag. Marinate up to one day in advance, keeping in refrigerator. Preheat oven to 375 degrees F and add potatoes, bake for 40-45 minutes, turn off heat when completed and keep warm in oven until ready to serve. Meanwhile, heat grill over medium high. Remove steak from bag and shake off excess marinade. Place steak over direct heat on the grill, cover and cook, turning once until internal temperature reaches 135 degrees F for medium rare/medium, 7-9 minutes depending on the size and cut. Remove from heat and allow the steak to rest for 3-4 minutes. Meanwhile, preheat a skillet over medium high heat and add 1 ½ tablespoons of butter. When butter begins to melt, add the entire bag of spinach and a pinch of kosher salt and black pepper. Sauté spinach until leaves have wilted and cooked down, about 2-3 minutes, and plate. Remove potatoes; make a small incision at the top of each, and season with salt and pepper. Top each potato with butter, sour cream, and chives; plate. Slice steak against the grain on the bias into ½ inch slices and plate, pouring any drippings over the sliced steak. Serve immediately.

Pimento Cheese Bruschetta

A southerner's take on an Italian staple. The pimento cheese can be made up to three days in advance and kept chilled and covered in the refrigerator. It should yield enough leftovers for a sandwich later in the week.

½ lb Sharp Cheddar Cheese, grated, at room temperature
2 Tablespoons Canned Diced Pimentos
2 Tablespoons Mayonnaise*
½ Loaf French Bread, cut into ½ inch slices
¼ Cup Extra Virgin Olive Oil*
Fresh Cracked Pepper*
2 Teaspoons Chives, finely chopped

Preheat oven to 400 degrees F. Combine the first three ingredients into a mixing bowl. Using a fork, mash ingredients until the cheese has softened and formed into a consistent mixture with the other ingredients, set aside. Lay out bread slices on a baking sheet and brush generously with olive oil and season with fresh cracked pepper. Place baking sheet in the oven and bake 6-8 minutes, until edges are golden brown. Remove from oven and spread a generous layer of the cheese mixture over the top of each piece of toasted bread. Garnish with chives and serve.

Savannah Cobb Salad

The classic Cobb salad done Savannah style. Take note that most of these ingredients must be pre-cooked prior to arrangement. Save some time and buy your shrimp, bacon, or eggs already prepared.

1 Heart of Romaine Lettuce, torn into bite sized pieces
¾ Cup Monterey Jack Cheese, grated
½ lb Cooked Large Pink Shrimp, peeled and cut in half
4 Strips Crispy Cooked Bacon, crumbled
¾ Cup Hard Boiled Eggs, peeled and roughly chopped
1 Vine Ripe Tomato, finely diced

¼ Medium Red Onion, finely diced
1 Avocado, seeded and diced
Naturally Fresh® Blue Cheese Dressing, or any other dressing of choice

Place lettuce in the bottom of a large serving bowl. Top lettuce with each remaining ingredient, as in creating slices of a pie for each separate ingredient. Serve with choice of dressing on the side.

Pan Seared Salmon with Parmesan Cream Cheese Grits and Roasted Okra

Pan searing the salmon will ensure maximum flavor and moisture. The Parmesan cream cheese grits and roasted okra help round out this meal of eclectic southern cuisine. Serve with Pinot Noir, Chardonnay, Riesling, Pale Ale, or Lager.

½ lb Fresh Okra, washed with ends removed
4 Tablespoons Extra Virgin Olive Oil, divided*
½ Teaspoon Cajun Seasoning*
3 ½ Cups Water
1 Cup Quick Cook Grits
2 Tablespoons Unsalted Butter
2 Tablespoons Parmigiano Reggiano Cheese, grated
¼ Cup Heavy Cream
2 6-8 oz Salmon Filets, skin removed
Kosher Salt*
Fresh Cracked Pepper*
Garlic Powder*
½ Lemon, juiced*
2 Teaspoons Red Bell Pepper, finely diced for garnish

Preheat oven to 350 degrees F. On a baking sheet, lay out okra in a single layer; drizzle with 2 tablespoons of oil and Cajun seasoning, toss to coat. Place okra on the top rack of the oven and roast for 25-30 minutes, turning on occasion. Bring 3 ½ cups of water to a boil in a small pot. Slowly add grits, butter, and ½ teaspoon of salt to the water. Stir until the mixture returns to a boil, ensuring an even consistency with no lumps. Reduce heat to medium-low, cover, and cook for 5-7 minutes, stirring on occasion until mixture is thick and water is incorporated. Add Parmigiano Reggiano cheese and heavy cream to grits and stir until well combined. Meanwhile, preheat a cast iron skillet over medium heat and season salmon filets with kosher salt, fresh cracked pepper, and garlic powder. Add 2 tablespoons of oil to the skillet followed by the salmon filets; cook, undisturbed, for 3-4 minutes. Squeeze the juice of ½ lemon over the top the filets; flip. Cook filets for 2-3 more minutes, or until internal temperature reaches 135 degrees F; remove from heat. Plate a generous portion of grits in the center of the plate, followed by the salmon and okra at either side. Sprinkle with diced red pepper for garnish. Serve immediately.

Antipasti Plate

This easy appetizer requires no cooking and can be quite versatile depending on your preferences. Feel free to substitute a meat or cheese of your choice. Most grocery stores feature an olive bar where you can find a nice variety of marinated olives. For a heartier appetizer, serve alongside some toasted Focaccia bread.

¼ lb Hard Salami, thinly sliced
¼ lb Aged Fontina Cheese, sliced
1 Cup Marinated Olives

On a serving platter, arrange slices of salami and cheese. Place olives in a smaller bowl and plate on top of the platter. Serve.

House Salad

Quick, light, and easy. This is just the right salad to refresh the palate after a heavy appetizer.

4 Cups Chopped Green Leaf Lettuce, loosely packed
6-8 Cherry Tomatoes
¼ Small Red Onion, thinly sliced
¼ Cup Extra Virgin Olive Oil*
1 ½ Tablespoons Red Wine Vinegar*
¼ Teaspoon Kosher Salt*
½ Teaspoon Fresh Cracked Pepper*
½ Teaspoon Italian Blend Seasoning*

Combine greens, tomatoes, and onions into a large serving bowl. In a separate mixing bowl, combine oil and vinegar, mix vigorously to combine ingredients. Pour the mixture over salad and season with salt, pepper, and Italian blend seasoning. Toss well and serve.

Shrimp and Mushroom Risotto

Risotto, at its best, is hard to beat. The secret is constant love and attention. Go ahead and knock out the other items on the menu and have them ready to go, because you will need to focus all of your attention on stirring the risotto to get that perfect creamy texture that still holds a firm bite. Serve with Chardonnay, Pinot Grigio, Sauvignon Blanc, or Lager.

4 Tablespoons Extra Virgin Olive Oil, divided*
1 lb Large Shrimp, peeled and deveined
Kosher Salt*
Fresh Cracked Pepper*
1 Medium Shallot, minced
2 Cloves Garlic, minced*
1 Teaspoon Herbs de Provence Seasoning*
8 oz Portobello Mushrooms, sliced
1 Cup Arborio Rice
½ Cup Dry White Wine (Pinot Grigio, Chardonnay, Sauvignon Blanc)
6 Cups Chicken Broth
1 Tablespoon Unsalted butter*
¼ Cup Heavy Cream
¼ Cup Parmigiano Reggiano Cheese, grated
1 Tablespoon Flat Leaf Parsley, finely chopped*

In a small pot over low heat, add chicken broth and heat until warm. Next, preheat a cast iron skillet over medium high heat, add 2 tablespoons of oil. Season shrimp with a pinch of kosher salt and fresh cracked pepper and add to skillet, sauté until shrimp are just pink, about 2-3 minutes. Remove shrimp from pan and set aside on a separate plate and tent with foil to keep warm. Add remaining 2 tablespoons of oil back into the skillet along with shallots, garlic, and Herbs de Provence seasoning; cook for 2-3 minutes. Add mushrooms and sauté until tender, about 4-5 minutes. Add rice into the skillet with the other ingredients and stir to coat the grains in oil. Cook for another 2-3 minutes, or until grains begin to become opaque. Add wine and bring to a simmer for 1-2 minutes. Reduce heat to medium and ladle in 1 cup of the warmed broth, stirring constantly with a wooden spoon until the rice has absorbed all of the liquid. Continue in this manner, 1 cup at a time, allowing the rice to absorb the liquid (All of the liquid may not be used). When mixture becomes slightly firm, yet still creamy (30-35 min), add the shrimp back in to finish cooking. Add butter, cream, and cheese; stir until well blended, 1-2 minutes. Remove from heat, plate, and serve. Garnish with finely chopped parsley.

The Special Occasion

Ok ... wait a second. Are you sure you want to go here? Remember that talk with your friends about whether or not she might be crazy? After these meals, she'll definitely be hooked for good, so make sure she's a keeper. If not, revert back to the weekday meals and keep her on standby. In all seriousness, by this point, I expect you to be pulling out all the stops; appetizers, salads, entrées, desserts, vintage wines, live jazz, etc. You get the idea. Remember all of that talk about you being in control? Sorry, she's got you by the balls now.

Shrimp Cocktail

Homemade cocktail sauce will always beat that stuff in the jar. If you need a shortcut, have your seafood department steam the shrimp for you while you shop for your other ingredients.

1 Tablespoon Cajun Seasoning*
1 Garlic Clove, crushed and peeled*
1 Lemon, cut in half*
1 lb Extra Large Pink Shrimp (U-10), deveined
4 Tablespoons Ketchup*
½ Teaspoon Horseradish
5-6 Fresh Sprigs Thyme, as garnish

Heat a 2 qt pot of water over medium high heat. As water begins to boil, add seasoning, garlic, and ½ of lemon. Add shrimp to the simmering water and cook until shrimp are pink and firm, about 4-5 minutes. Immediately strain the shrimp through a colander and place in the refrigerator to cool, or an ice bath if serving immediately. In a small mixing bowl, combine ketchup, horseradish, and the juice from the remaining lemon ½, mix until well combined. Remove cooled shrimp and peel the body portion of the shell away from the meat, leaving the tail on. Serve chilled, placing shrimp around martini glasses with a serving of the homemade cocktail sauce in the bottom of the glass. Place thyme springs vertically on top of the cocktail sauce for garnish.

Wedge Salad

One of my favorites for its simplicity and unique presentation.

½ Head Iceberg lettuce, core removed and cut in half
4 Strips Crispy Cooked Bacon, crumbled
1 Roma Tomato, seeded and finely diced
2 Teaspoons Green Onion Tops, finely chopped
Naturally Fresh® Blue Cheese Dressing
Fresh Cracked Pepper, to garnish*

Place a lettuce quarter on each serving plate. Drizzle each with blue cheese dressing. Top with equal portions of crumbled bacon, tomatoes, and chives. Using 2-3 turns of a peppermill, crack fresh pepper on top of salad for garnish.

DATE #16

Grilled Hanger Steak with Roasted Potatoes and Balsamic Grilled Onions

The best part of this meal is that everything goes on the grill. This makes for easy cleanup, leaving you plenty of time to drink a few beers (gain courage) while manning the fire. Be sure to pay special attention to my cues of direct and indirect heat in the recipe. Pair with Cabernet, Merlot, Pale Ale, or Stout. Man created fire, so act like you know what you are doing.

1 Cup Extra Virgin Olive Oil*
2 Tablespoons Balsamic Vinegar*
4 Tablespoons Fresh Lemon Juice, divided*
2 Cloves Garlic, thinly sliced*
1 Large 12-16 oz Hanger or Flank Steak
2 Medium Red Onions, sliced into ½ inch rings
Kosher Salt*
Fresh Cracked Pepper*
2 lbs Red New Potatoes, scrubbed and quartered
2 Teaspoons Fresh Rosemary, coarsely chopped

At least one hour before grilling, add ½ cup of oil, balsamic vinegar, 2 tablespoons of lemon juice, and garlic into a large Ziploc® bag. Season steak and onions liberally with salt and pepper and add to bag. Marinate up to one day in advance, keeping in refrigerator. Heat grill over medium high. Using two large sheets of aluminum foil, lay out and season potatoes with salt and pepper, ½ cup of olive oil, 2 tablespoons of lemon juice, and rosemary. Fold foil to create a seamless pouch and place on a covered grill over indirect heat for 40-45 minutes. Remove onions from bag and place on the grill over direct heat, turning once, cooking for 2-3 minutes per side. Move onions to indirect heat, cooking for an additional 12-15 minutes. Remove steak from bag and shake off excess marinade. Grill covered and undisturbed over direct heat, turning once until internal temperature reaches 135 degrees F for medium rare/medium, about 7-9 minutes depending on the size and cut. Remove the steak from the heat and allow it to rest for 3-4 minutes. Remove potatoes (careful when opening foil) and onions from the grill and plate. Slice the steak against the grain and on the bias into ½ inch slices and plate, pouring any remaining drippings on top of the sliced steak. Serve immediately.

Grilled Peaches with Vanilla Ice Cream

Keep on grilling on. Save time and effort, and leave the grill on low while eating to cook off and clean the grate. Have the peaches sliced and cleaned in advance to get this dessert out quickly after eating dinner.

1 Tablespoon Unsalted Butter
2 Teaspoons Brown Sugar
½ Teaspoon Ground Cinnamon
2 Medium Ripe Peaches, halved with pits removed
6 oz Vanilla Ice Cream

In a small microwave safe mixing bowl, combine butter, brown sugar, and cinnamon. Place the bowl in the microwave for 30 seconds on high, mix well. Using a sharp knife, carefully cut all the way around the side of the peaches and twist to remove the pits, using a spoon to dig out the pits if needed. On a lightly greased grill over medium high heat, place the peaches cut side down and cook for 3-4 minutes. Turn over peaches, generously spread with the sugar and cinnamon mixture, and move to indirect heat, cover and cook, 10-12 minutes. Remove peaches from grill and serve in individual bowls immediately with equal portions of vanilla ice cream.

Crab Cakes with Remoulade

Crab Cakes should be just that, crab. This recipe doesn't add a whole lot of filler, and allows the sweet and delicate crabmeat to shine. The remoulade is a great accompaniment to this classic.

Remoulade:

½ Cup Mayonnaise*
½ Lemon, juiced*
1 Clove Garlic, finely minced*
1 Tablespoon Whole Grain Mustard*
1 Teaspoon Capers, minced
1 Teaspoon Chives, finely chopped
1 Dash Tabasco® Hot Sauce

Combine all ingredients into a small mixing bowl and whisk until thoroughly incorporated. Cover and chill in the refrigerator until ready to serve, keeps up to 2 days. Serve on the side of the crab cakes.

Crab Cakes:

1 lb Jumbo Lump Crabmeat, picked free of shells
½ Cup Bread Crumbs
1 Teaspoon Chives, finely chopped
¼ Cup Red Bell Pepper, finely diced
¼ Cup Mayonnaise*
½ Lemon, juiced*
1 Egg*
1 Teaspoon Whole Grain Mustard*
¼ Teaspoon Salt*
4 Tablespoons Extra Virgin Olive Oil*

Combine all ingredients, with the exception of the oil, into a large mixing bowl and shape into patties about the size of your palm, yielding about 4 cakes in total. Add oil to a preheated cast iron skillet over medium heat. Add cakes and cook 3-4 minutes. Carefully flip and cook for another 2-3 minutes. Serve with remoulade on the side.

DATE #17

Caprese Salad

Fresh ingredients are the key to this favorite. The stacked presentation makes for a creative and easy assembly, but be sure to include a knife to go along with serving this one.

4 Vine Ripe Tomatoes, sliced
Kosher Salt*
8 oz Fresh Mozzarella Cheese, sliced
8-10 Fresh Basil leaves*
2 Teaspoons Extra Virgin Olive Oil, divided*
1 Teaspoon Balsamic Vinegar, divided*
Fresh Cracked Pepper*

Lightly season tomato slices with kosher salt. On two serving plates, begin with a slice of tomato followed by a slice of mozzarella. Continue with 2-3 layers of the tomato and cheese stack arrangement. On a cutting board, stack and roll basil leaves together, and using a chef's knife, thinly slice the leaves, or chiffonade. Arrange the sliced basil on top of the stacked tomato and cheese. Drizzle each stack with 1 teaspoon of olive oil and ½ teaspoon of vinegar. Garnish with a few turns of fresh cracked pepper.

Pan Seared Scallops with Red Pepper Cream over Orzo Pasta

Orzo is a rice shaped pasta that can be found right alongside traditional pastas in the grocery store. The U-10 description on the scallops refers to a quantity of 10 per pound, or about 5 per person. Use a paper towel to pat the scallops dry. Moisture will prevent the scallops from having that nice caramelized sear. Pair with Chardonnay, Pinot Noir, or Amber Ale.

1 Cup Heavy Cream
½ Teaspoon Cajun Seasoning
1 12 oz Jar Roasted Red Peppers, drained and cleaned of seeds
1 Clove Garlic, crushed*
1 Teaspoon Fresh Lemon Juice*
1 Cup Orzo Pasta
Kosher Salt*
Fresh Cracked Pepper*
1 lb (U-10) Large Sea Scallops, patted dry
2 Tablespoons Extra Virgin Olive Oil*
¼ Cup Parmigiano Reggiano Cheese, grated
1 Teaspoon Chives, finely chopped.

Add cream and Cajun seasoning to a Dutch oven or heavy bottomed pot and bring to a slow simmer over medium low heat, careful not to burn, 25-30 minutes, stirring on occasion. Next, heat a large pot of water over high heat. Combine the roasted red peppers, garlic, and lemon juice into a food processor or blender and puree for 20-30 seconds, or until all ingredients are combined. Add the roasted red pepper puree into the simmering cream and whisk thoroughly. When water comes to a boil, add orzo pasta and cook 6-7 minutes, or al dente. Drain orzo into a colander and set aside. In the meantime, preheat a cast iron skillet over medium high heat. Season scallops with salt and fresh cracked pepper. Add oil to skillet, followed by the scallops and cook undisturbed for 2-3 minutes, flip and continue to cook for another 1-2 minutes, or until scallops are firm to the touch. Add the Parmigiano Reggiano cheese into the red pepper cream, whisk thoroughly, and remove from heat. Taste red pepper cream and adjust seasoning as necessary. Plate the orzo, followed by a generous ladle of the warm red pepper cream over the top. Top with equal portions of seared scallops. Garnish with chives and serve immediately.

Yogurt and Fruit Parfait

A light and quick dessert that's perfect for any occasion. Most grocers will carry a pint of mixed berries already washed and prepared for you in the produce section. Any combination of berries listed below will be perfect. This can be put together very quickly, so don't worry about preparing this in advance. Otherwise, the granola will become soggy.

2 Cups Vanilla Nonfat Yogurt
1 Pint Fresh Mixed Berries (Strawberries, Blackberries, Raspberries, and Blueberries)
1 Cup Bear Naked® Fruit and Nut Granola

In two separate tall glasses; start off with a layer of a quarter cup of yogurt at the bottom of each glass. Follow with a layer of fruit and then granola. Continue this pattern until glasses are filled to the top. Garnish with an extra sprinkle of granola on top. Serve immediately.

Grilled Italian Sausage with Whole Grain Mustard

Easy and quick. Try the hot versions of Italian sausage to spice things up. Substitute Andouille, Kielbasa, or any other favorite grilling sausage when desired.

2 Links Fresh Ground Mild Italian Sausage
2 Tablespoons Whole Grain Mustard*
2 Teaspoons Green Onion Tops, sliced as garnish
Toothpicks to serve

Preheat grill over medium high heat. Add sausages and cook, turning on occasion, 10-12 minutes or until internal temperature reaches 160 degrees F. Remove, and allow to rest 1-2 minutes. Slice sausages on the bias and place around the perimeter of a serving plate with the mustard in the center. Garnish with green onion tops. Serve.

Mandarin Salad

This salad provides a nice serving of citrus to help clean the palate after a heavy appetizer. The flavors of this dish will help set the stage for the pork tenderloin served later in the meal.

4 Cups Pre-Washed Spring Mix Salad, loosely packed
½ Cup Canned Mandarin Oranges, drained, liquid reserved
1 Teaspoon Chives, finely chopped
2 Tablespoons Almonds, sliced
¼ Cup Extra Virgin Olive Oil*

1 Tablespoon Reserved Mandarin Orange Liquid
1 Tablespoon Balsamic Vinegar*
1 Pinch Kosher Salt*
¼ Teaspoon Fresh Cracked Pepper*

Arrange the spring mix salad in the bottom of a large serving bowl. Top with mandarin oranges, chives, and almonds. In a separate mixing bowl, combine oil, reserved liquid, vinegar, salt, and pepper. Whisk together ingredients until combined. Pour dressing over salad, toss and serve.

Grilled Pork Tenderloin with Roasted Potatoes and Sautéed Zucchini

Often considered the filet mignon of the pork world, this cut is extra tender and juicy. Pair with Zinfandel, Pinot Noir, Merlot, Amber Ale, or Pale Ale.

1 Cup Extra Virgin Olive Oil, plus 2 tablespoons*
¼ Cup Soy Sauce*
2 Cloves Garlic, minced*
1 Medium 16-20 oz. Pork Tenderloin, trimmed of fat
Kosher Salt*
Fresh Cracked Pepper*
2 lbs Red New Potatoes, scrubbed and quartered
2 Tablespoons Fresh Lemon Juice*
2 Teaspoons Fresh Rosemary
1 lb Zucchini, washed and thinly sliced

At least one hour before grilling, add ½ cup of oil, soy sauce, and garlic into a large Ziploc® bag. Season the tenderloin lightly with salt and pepper and add to bag. Marinate up to one day in advance, keeping in refrigerator. Heat grill over medium. Preheat oven to 400 degrees F. In a large baking dish, season potatoes with salt and pepper, ½ cup of olive oil, 2 tablespoons of lemon juice, and rosemary. Place potatoes in the oven and roast until fork tender, about 35-40 minutes. Meanwhile, add the tenderloin to the grill and cook covered, turning often, until internal temperature reaches 145-150 degrees F, or 20-25 minutes depending on the size and cut. About 10 minutes before serving, heat a large skillet over medium high heat with 2 tablespoons of oil. Season zucchini with salt and pepper and add to skillet. Cook 4-5 minutes until zucchini are tender and slightly browned. Remove the tenderloin from the grill, and allow it to rest 4-5 minutes. Slice the tenderloin on the bias every ½ inch and plate. Remove potatoes from the oven and plate next to the sliced tenderloin and sautéed zucchini. Serve.

Baked Apples

This dessert works great when the apples are prepared in advance, and then placed in the oven while eating dinner. The aromas of the apples and cinnamon will surely heighten anticipation for what's to come. Pair this with vanilla ice cream if you desire.

2 Large Apples, Golden Delicious or Granny Smith
4 Tablespoons Unsalted Butter, in 1 tablespoon increments*
2 Teaspoons Brown Sugar
½ Teaspoon Ground Cinnamon

Preheat oven to 350 degrees F. Wash and dry apples, slice in half, remove core and seeds using a spoon or knife. In a Pyrex baking dish, carefully arrange apples flesh side up. Sprinkle evenly with brown sugar and cinnamon and top each half with 1 tablespoon of butter. Bake until apples are tender and bubbly, about 30-35 minutes. Remove apples from baking dish and plate 2 halves on each serving plate. Drizzle any remaining butter or juices over the top before serving.

Ciabatta Crostinis

These can be made up to one day in advance and can be served either hot or cold on the side of the salad or the entrée. You could also pair these with some warmed marinara for a simple appetizer.

½ Loaf Ciabatta Bread
¼ Extra Virgin Olive Oil*
Fresh Cracked Pepper*
1 Clove Garlic, peeled and cut in half*
½ Cup Parmigiano Reggiano Cheese, grated

Preheat oven to 400 degrees F. Slice the loaf at an angle, every ½ inch or so, into toasts. Generously brush each toast with olive oil and fresh cracked pepper. Add toasts to a baking sheet and bake 10-12 minutes until crispy and dry, remove from oven. Lightly rub the cut side of the garlic on the surface of each piece of toasted bread. Next, lightly top each crostini with Parmigiano Reggiano cheese, return to oven for 1-2 minutes until cheese is bubbly and slightly browned. Remove from heat and set aside to cool.

Toasted Pine Nut and Arugula Salad

Toasting the pine nuts helps release the natural oils, bringing out the earthy flavor of this beloved nut. This salad is best served when the pine nuts are still slightly warm.

¼ **Cup Pine Nuts**
4 Cups Pre-Washed Arugula, loosely packed
1 ½ Tablespoons Balsamic Vinegar*
¼ **Cup Extra Virgin Olive Oil***

¼ **Teaspoon Kosher Salt***
2 oz Crumbled Blue or Gorgonzola Cheese

Preheat oven to 400 degrees F. On a baking sheet, lay out pine nuts in a single layer. Toast in oven 3-4 minutes, shaking often and careful not to burn. Combine the toasted pine nuts with the arugula in a large serving bowl. In a separate container whisk together; vinegar, oil, and salt until incorporated. Drizzle dressing over greens and toss lightly until leaves are coated. Top with crumbled blue cheese.

Braised Beef over Egg Noodles

Braising can turn humble cuts of meat into succulent and tender pieces that fall right off the bone. The aromas of this dish cooking during the day will set the mood for a romantic evening. Pair with a Côtes du Rhône, Merlot, or Cabernet. This recipe will definitely yield leftovers for later in the week.

¼ **Cup Extra Virgin Olive Oil***
1 3 lb Boneless Beef Chuck Roast
Kosher Salt*
Fresh Cracked Pepper*
2 Cups Yellow Onions, roughly chopped
1 Cup Carrots, roughly chopped
1 Cup Celery, roughly chopped
2 Cups Button Mushrooms, sliced
2 Cloves Garlic, minced*
1 Bottle Red Wine
3 Cups Beef Broth
2 Bay Leaves
1 lb Wide Egg Noodles
6 Tablespoons Unsalted Butter, divided*
3 Tablespoons All Purpose Flour
2 Teaspoons Fresh Parsley, chopped for garnish*

Preheat a Dutch oven or a large heavy bottomed pot over medium high heat, add oil. Liberally season roast with kosher salt and fresh cracked pepper. Add roast to the pan and brown on all sides, about 1-2 minutes per side, remove from pan and set aside. Add onions, carrots, and celery and cook 10-12 minutes, or until tender. Add mushrooms, garlic, and roast back into the pot, on top of the softened vegetables. Next, add the wine and broth, up to 1 inch below the top of the roast. Bring to a boil. Reduce heat to medium low, add bay leaves, cover, and simmer until beef is tender, about 2 ½ - 3 hours. Remove roast from pan and tent with foil to keep warm. On the Dutch oven, increase the heat to medium-high to reduce the cooking liquid, about 10-15 minutes, remove bay leaves. In a separate pot of salted water over high heat, boil egg noodles until al dente, 8-10 minutes. Meanwhile, in a small pan over medium heat, melt 3 tablespoons of butter into 3 tablespoons of flour and whisk for 4-5 minutes to create a light roux. Add the roux mixture into the Dutch oven with the reduced cooking liquid, whisk thoroughly, and remove from heat to cool and thicken. Remove egg noodles from heat and drain; return to the same pot and mix in remaining 3 tablespoons of butter until melted, plate. Thinly slice the beef across the grain and plate on top of noodles. Generously ladle thickened sauce and vegetables on top of the beef and noodles. Garnish with parsley. Serve.

Toasted Walnuts and Chocolate Ice Cream

This simple dessert will pair nicely with the deep and rich flavors from the braised beef. Keep that glass of Merlot or Cabernet on the table, as the notes in the wine will work perfectly with the chocolate and nutty flavor in this dessert.

¼ Cup Walnuts, chopped
6 oz Chocolate Ice Cream
Hershey's® Chocolate Syrup, if desired

Preheat a cast iron skillet over medium heat. Add walnuts and toast 3-4 minutes. Meanwhile, divide the ice cream into two serving bowls. Remove walnuts from skillet, and top each bowl with a generous serving around the ice cream. Garnish with a drizzle of chocolate syrup if desired. Serve.

Bacon Wrapped Sea Scallops

The saltiness of the bacon combined with the sweet scallop is a combination that's hard to beat. These also work great on the grill. Don't let the bacon cool for too long, otherwise it will stiffen, making it difficult to wrap around the scallop.

6 Slices Thick Cut Bacon
6 (U-10 size) Sea Scallops, patted dry
6 (6 inch) Bamboo Skewers
2 Tablespoons Extra Virgin Olive Oil*
Fresh Cracked Pepper*

Preheat oven to 400 degrees F. On a baking sheet, lay out the bacon slices in a single layer and cook in the oven for 9-12 minutes, making sure the slices are still pliable. Remove the bacon from the oven and allow to cool briefly on paper towels. Wrap each scallop with a slice of bacon, securing the bacon by placing a skewer through the center of the wrap. Preheat a cast iron skillet over medium high heat, add oil, followed by the scallops. Cook scallops, turning once, for 2-3 minutes on each side. Garnish with fresh cracked pepper. Serve.

Caesar Salad

Be adventurous here and give the homemade dressing a try. If you are cramped for time, this whole salad can be simplified with store-bought croutons and dressing (Ken's® Caesar dressing is recommended).

Dressing

2 Cloves Garlic, minced fine *
2 Anchovy Filets, minced fine
¼ Teaspoon Kosher Salt *
1 Egg *
1 Lemon, juiced *
1 Teaspoon Balsamic Vinegar *
¼ Cup Finely Grated Parmigiano Reggiano Cheese
½ Teaspoon Fresh Cracked Pepper *
¼ Cup Extra Virgin Olive Oil *

On a cutting board, combine the minced garlic, anchovies, and kosher salt. Using a chef's knife, work ingredients into a paste on the board. Combine paste, egg, lemon juice, and balsamic vinegar into a large mixing bowl or food processor and mix vigorously for at least one minute, until mixture is smooth and almost beige in color. Add cheese and pepper and mix for another 30 seconds. Continue to mix and slowly stream in olive oil at the same time, to combine, or emulsify. Serve, or keep the dressing in the refrigerator until ready, up to 2 days.

Salad/Croutons

½ Loaf French Bread, cut into bite sized cubes
4 Tablespoons Extra Virgin Olive Oil *
Kosher Salt *
Fresh Cracked Pepper *
1 Heart of Romaine Lettuce, torn into bite size pieces
2 oz Shaved Parmigiano Reggiano Cheese

Preheat oven to 400 degrees F. On a baking sheet, lay out the French bread cubes in a single layer. Drizzle with olive oil and season with salt and pepper to taste. Toss the bread cubes to coat evenly with oil and place in the oven for 10-12 minutes, until cubes are crisp. Allow croutons to cool. In a large serving bowl, combine the lettuce and dressing and toss to coat the leaves. Add the croutons and cheese. Top with dressing and serve.

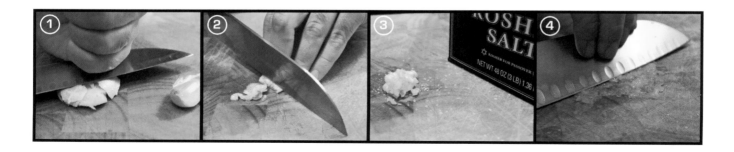

Filet Mignon with Asparagus and Garlic Mashed Potatoes

Don't hold back on the cut of meat on this one. The other ingredients are fairly inexpensive, so invest in some quality filets. Pair with Merlot, Syrah, or Cabernet.

2 lbs Red New Potatoes, peeled and quartered
3 Garlic Cloves, peeled*
½ lb Fresh Asparagus, trimmed and cleaned
4 Tablespoons Extra Virgin Olive Oil, extra for garnish*
2 8-10 oz Filet Mignons, at room temperature
Kosher Salt *
Fresh Cracked Pepper*
6 Tablespoons Unsalted Butter*
¼ Cup Heavy Cream

Preheat the oven to 425 degrees F. Heat a large pot of water over medium high heat. When water comes to a boil, add potatoes and garlic cloves and cook 11-13 minutes, or until fork tender; remove from heat and set aside. Next, lay out asparagus in a single layer on a baking sheet; drizzle with 2 tablespoons of oil, season with salt and pepper, and toss to coat each spear. Meanwhile, heat a cast iron skillet over medium high heat and season filets with salt and pepper. Add 2 tablespoons of oil followed by the filets; cook, undisturbed, for 3-4 minutes. Flip filets, and insert into the bottom rack of the oven until internal temperature is 135 degrees F for medium rare/medium, about 5-7 more minutes depending on the cut. Next, place asparagus on the top rack of a 425 degree oven, cook 10-12 minutes. Drain potatoes and allow steam to evaporate. Melt the butter and cream in a small pot over low heat. Using a potato ricer or masher, mash potatoes and garlic into a mixing bowl. Mix in the butter and cream with potatoes and season to taste with kosher salt, and fresh cracked pepper. Remove filets from oven and allow the filets to rest while plating. Plate a large heaping of potatoes in the center of the plate. Next, rest the asparagus at a vertical angle, on the side of the potatoes; carefully angle the filet on the asparagus. Lightly drizzle olive oil on top to garnish.

Chocolate Covered Strawberries

Make it easy, and prepare these in advance. They will keep for up to 2 days in the refrigerator.

2 Tablespoons Unsalted Butter
10 oz Semisweet Chocolate, chopped
1 lb Fresh Strawberries, washed and dried thoroughly

Fill a two quart pot with 2-3 inches of water and bring to a simmer over medium high heat. Place butter and chocolate into a separate heatproof medium bowl and carefully rest it inside of the pot with the simmering water. Remove pot from heat and allow chocolate to slowly melt in the bowl, stirring on occasion. Holding the stem, dip each strawberry into the melted chocolate, ensuring an even coat, and place on a baking sheet lined with wax or parchment paper. Continue until all strawberries have been dipped, or no chocolate remains. Set the strawberries aside for at least 30 minutes, to allow the chocolate to set; or keep in the fridge until ready to serve.

AUTHOR MATT MOORE resides in the Germantown Historic District of Nashville, TN. In addition to writing and cooking, he is a performing country music singer/songwriter. Other hobbies include running, traveling, fishing, and drinking cold beer with friends and strangers.

ACKNOWLEDGMENTS

THE AUTHOR WOULD LIKE TO THANK, FIRST AND FOREMOST, MY FAMILY, AND ESPECIALLY MY MOTHER, FOR THEIR CREATIVE SUPPORT AND DIRECTION WHILE WRITING THIS BOOK. A special thanks to all of the friends who replicated, sampled, and provided feedback on all of the recipes in this book. Specifically, I would like to acknowledge the following people:

Emily Breland - Editing
Caroline Cutbirth - Modeling
Mary Elizabeth Hulsey – Set Design
Paige Rumore - Photography
Jill Townsend - Graphic Design
Charlie Holderness - Logo and Marketing
Jeff Krones - Creative Artists Agency

In memory of my loving grandmother, the best cook I've ever known.
Blanche "Sitty" Dennis

LaVergne, TN USA
18 November 2009
164532LV00001B